DOWSING FOR HEALTH AND HARMONY

Dowsing for Health And Harmony

Copyright © 2021 by Chris Pisani.

Paperback ISBN: 978-1-63812-026-1
Ebook ISBN: 978-1-63812-027-8

All rights reserved. No part in this book may be produced and transmitted in any form or by any means, electronic, or mechanical, including photocopying, recording, or by any information storage and retrieval system, without permission in writing from the copyright owner.

The views expressed in this work are solely those of the author and do not necessarily reflect the views of the publisher hereby disclaims any responsibility for them.

Published by Pen Culture Solutions   05/16/2021

Pen Culture Solutions
1-888-727-7204 (USA)
1-800-950-458 (Australia)
support@penculturesolutions.com

TABLE OF CONTENTS

Introduction	Pages 1 & 2
Ways of Dowsing	3
Dowsing with a Pendulum – Introduction	4
Dowsing with Divining Rods – Introduction	5
Getting to know your Pendulum	6 - 10
Working with your Pendulum	11 - 14
Dowsing your food	15 - 16
Working with other people	17 - 19
Working with Chakras	20 - 27
Dowsing for Health and Harmony	28 - 31
Other areas for Dowsing	32
Dowsing with Rods	33 - 35
Dowsing for Energy fields	36 - 45
Dowsing for Geopathic Stress	46 - 50
Finale	51
Bodies to practice on	52 - 53

You are here because you are on a journey.

Maybe there was something in your life that you weren't happy with. Maybe you had a feeling inside that there was more to life than what you were experiencing.

No matter what reason, your journey has brought you here.

We at our Craigmore Sanctuary in South Australia are on a journey also.

Our Spiritual Guides have directed us to this property, and asked that we build for them a Sanctuary so that we can pass knowledge on to all who seek.

This knowledge has been given to us not only by trial and error, but by experience and by the teachings of those who Guide us.

Our journey is to teach. Your journey is to learn. Not only from us, but from those beautiful Spiritual Beings who surround you. Learn to listen to what feels right for you. You will be guided unerringly in this. If what you hear does not feel right for you, then move on.

You will hear many things over the years, some knowledge you will retain, other knowledge you will disregard. It doesn't matter if you don't follow the same path as your friends and companions.

Follow the path of truth and love, asking always for the Highest and Best available to you at this point in time and you will know that your path is the right one for you.

The knowledge we impart to you will hopefully assist you in finding your pathway in life.

Perhaps our information is at odds with other teachers, but we know that we have been guided in our learning, and our teaching is monitored by Higher Beings than ourselves, therefore we can only impart to you what we ourselves have learned.

We hope your journey will be beautiful. We know from our own experience that it can be painful. We know also, that you will struggle between the physical and the Spiritual.

Let us hope that we can assist you with this struggle, and bring to you the Love, the Joy and the knowledge that we as physical beings are well loved by the Spiritual Realm.

Allow yourselves to feel the guidance of the Spiritual Realm in your everyday lives and have trust in this guidance.

If we have been able to assist you on your journey then we too have been assisted on our own.

May the Light of The Great Spirit shine down upon you.

There are a number of different ways of Dowsing. This course covers two.

(a) The use of a Pendulum
(b) The use of Divining Rods.

Warning:

We do not proscribe the use of either tools as a means of Fortune Telling or for use as an Oracle.

Dowsing With A Pendulum:

1. Dowsing with a Pendulum when used for Healing purposes is an early means of tuning in to Spiritual Guidance.

2. It is a tool that will help your Healing Guides assist you in finding and balancing the energy centres in your body (chakras), and places of injury or pain and disruptions within the energy field of the body. The more you use this tool, the more sensitive you will become, the closer your link with your Healing Guides, and eventually the Pendulum will become redundant.

3. Dowsing for literature in Libraries and book stores, dowsing your food, health food products, kitchen cleaning chemicals, naturopathic remedies and many other items, will enable you to find what is suitable for you at that point in time.

Dowsing With Divining Rods:

1. Dowsing with Divining Rods will assist you in finding areas of Geopathic Stress which can cause illness and disharmony within the home.

2. Home maintenance can be assisted by using the Divining Rods to find structural faults, plumbing problems, water leaks and blockages, in fact to find water pipes themselves.

3. Divining Rods can assist in decisions about property purchase by discovering underground water or unhealthy energy lines. As a tool, the Divining Rod will remain with you as long as you choose to use it.

We hope that this course will start you on a Spiritual Journey of investigation to help both yourself and your fellow man as well as to assist in the healing of Mother Earth.

GETTING TO KNOW YOUR PENDULUM

There are many different types of Pendulums.

1. A Crystal.
2. A split pin.
3. A piece of jewellery.

In fact any object that can be placed on a piece of string or cotton, or can hang suspended, can be used as a Pendulum.

Because we hope that your Pendulum will become a treasured and protected article, we suggest that a small crystal be used, and carried with you on your person so it absorbs your energy and becomes easier to use.

(As with all crystals, we do not recommend allowing others to handle yours and also recommend occasional cleaning and clearing by the use of a salt water bath)

Getting to know your Pendulum Cont/..

Crystals have a memory, and by using a crystal as a Pendulum it will remember it's function.

Dowsing for Health and Harmony requires a certain state of mind. This state of mind is transferred to the Pendulum, so remember when handling your crystal to be reverent and especially sincere and honest as ultimately you are connecting with your Spiritual Guides.

Hold the crystal within your hands. Open your mind gently and connect lovingly with your crystal. Rub it gently between your hands so it absorbs your vibration and program it thus:

"I………………………….. the user of this Pendulum, ask of God Almighty (or The Great Spirit or whichever name you choose to call the Creator) to be protected from all evil and deception and that the answers that I am given by this Pendulum be always The Truth and nothing but The Truth and within the range of my understanding".

"I ask that my Guides and Helpers stand close to enable me to understand the answers that I am given and to guide me in asking the correct questions"

Getting to know your Pendulum Cont/..

"I...........................the user of this Pendulum promise to use my Pendulum only for the highest and the best intentions and for my highest good"

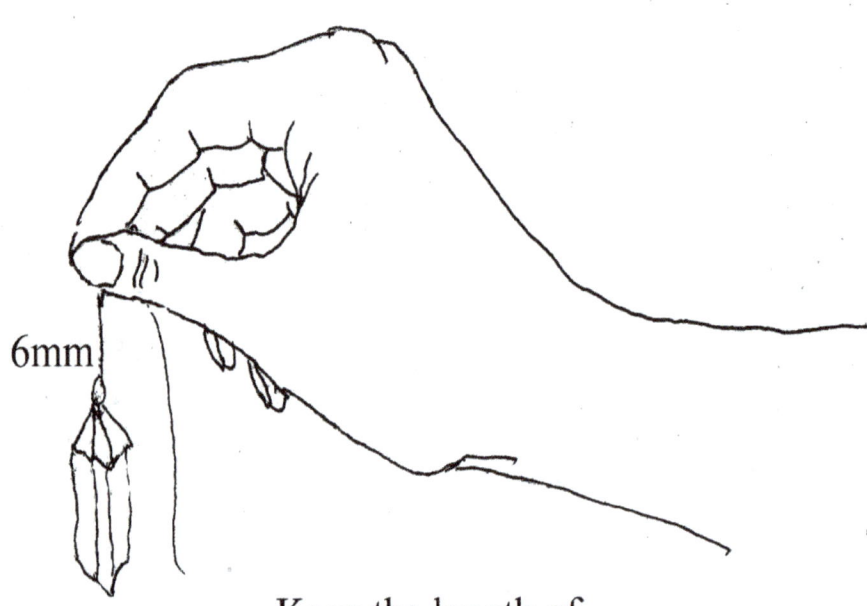

Keep the length of your cord short

Support wrist with other hand to there is no unintentional movement.

Getting to know your Pendulum Cont/..

If you are unable to get your Pendulum to move, we suggest that you hold the Pendulum over the diagram on the next page and move the Pendulum slightly yourself, and say to the Pendulum, *"This is what I want you to show me for ……………."*

Now it is necessary to understand just how your Pendulum will react to your questions.

1. Depending on whether you are left or right handed, hold the pendulum in your hand, supporting your wrist with your other hand.
2. Ask the Pendulum to show you **"SEARCH"**
3. Ask the Pendulum to show you **"YES"**
4. Ask the Pendulum to show you **"NO"**
5. Ask the Pendulum to show you **"CANNOT ANSWER"**

Not everybody will receive the same reaction from their Pendulum. That does not matter because the answers that you are receiving are personal to your vibration.

The typical answers are:-
1. Swinging VERY GENTLY backwards and forwards (about .1/2") for **"SEARCH"**
2. Circling anticlockwise for **"YES"**
3. Swinging backwards and forwards - about 2" – 3" (approx 6mm) for **"NO"**
4. Hovering between a circular movement and backwards and forwards movement for **"CANNOT ANSWER"** similar to the 'SEARCH' movement.

Fig 1.   Search
         (This is the motion used
         when you are looking
         for something)

Fig 2.   Yes and No

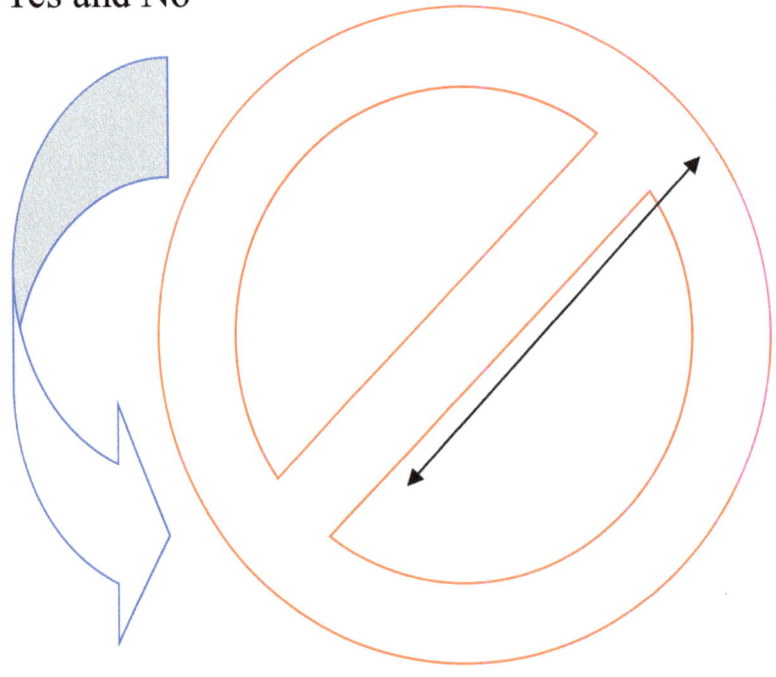

Fig 3.   Cannot Answer

Spend some time for you and your Pendulum to become acquainted.

WORKING WITH YOUR PENDULUM

Now that you and your Pendulum have become acquainted, it is now time to start working with it. It is important to remember that you MUST ask a simple question before you are given an answer of either **YES** or **NO**, or **CANNOT ANSWER**.

IF YOU INFLUENCE THE MOVEMENT OF YOUR PENDULUM YOURSELF, YOU ARE ONLY FOOLING YOURSELF.

Allow your Pendulum to give you an accurate answer. Moving your own hand to make the Pendulum move is not allowing the Spiritual energy to provide you with accurate answers.

Understand that it takes a great deal of practice with your Pendulum before you make a comfortable team. Your Pendulum needs to be carried with you and used often.

The most common mistake in receiving either no response or "**CANNOT ANSWER**" is asking the incorrect question.

Word your questions carefully, ensuring that they cannot be misinterpreted (e.g. "Can I check for water leaks in my pipes?" Of course you can, either with a plumber or by hand. But when? Today, tomorrow, or next week? The question should rather be "May I check for water leaks in my plumbing now? If the answer is "**YES**" go ahead.

Working with your Pendulum cont/..

If the answer is "**NO**" there must be a good reason for that answer. Have faith in the outcome.

I cannot stress strongly enough the three things that must be asked each time you work with your Pendulum.

THEY ARE:

Can I?

May I?

Should I?

It might seem strange that you should ask these three questions, but there are times when it is not appropriate for you to receive an answer to your question.

You might ask, "Then what is the use of me having a Pendulum?" The answer is, **when the answer is to your highest good.**

Remember to be especially specific in your statements or you will get a "**CANNOT ANSWER**" response.

If you are going to check on another persons food or medication. If your question is of a personal nature. No matter what the question, you must first ask permission.

You must make the statement "I WISH TO CHECK THE …………………..OF ………….."

Working with your Pendulum cont/..

Can I?

Well after getting to know your Pendulum and understanding its responses you will most probably get a "**YES**" answer to this question. If however, you get a "**NO**" response, you will know that at that point in time your expertise does not extend to that level.

May I?

Asking this question clarifies whether it is appropriate for you to find out this information.

If you get a "**YES**" answer to this question you know that it is. If you get a "**NO**" answer to this question, you know that it is not.

Do not be offended if you get a "**NO**" answer. There may be something that you are not aware of, or you may be asking a frivolous question. There are many reasons why this answer is received.

Should I?

This may sound like you are repeating the last question in a different way, but I assure you, you are not.

There are many reasons why you would receive a "**YES**" answer to the previous two questions, and a "**NO**" answer to this last one. Perhaps you are not ready to hear the information that you will find out. Whatever the reason, respect the answers to your questions.

Working with your Pendulum cont/..

If you have received all "**YES'S**", double check your answers by asking: "**AM I CORRECT IN MY UNDERSTANDING THAT I HAVE RECEIVED THE ANSWER YES TO ALL MY QUESTIONS?**"

If the answer is "**YES**", then you can start work.

DOWSING YOUR FOOD

This might seem like a strange thing to do, but with today's hectic lifestyle, much of our food is pre-prepared, over processed and filled with artificial substances that may or may not cause problems with our health.

Some processed foods have been so refined that they no longer contain sufficient nutrients for our body's needs.

Some of the foods that we dearly love, could actually be causing havoc to our systems. Foods such as Icecream, Milk, Sugar, Chocolate, Fried Chips, even such things as our breakfast cereal.

Would it not then be wise, to set out your favourite foods, remembering to ask the following:

"I………………………….. the user of this Pendulum, ask of God Almighty (or The Great Spirit or whichever name you choose to call the Creator) to be protected from all evil and deception and that the answers that I am given by this Pendulum be always The Truth and nothing but The Truth and within the range of my understanding.

"I ask that my Guides and Helpers stand close to enable me to understand the answers that I am given and to guide me in asking the correct questions"

"I………………………….the user of this Pendulum promise to use my Pendulum only for the highest and the best intentions and for my highest good"

Dowsing your Food cont/..

In preparing to get a response from your Pendulum, you must ask a question that you required answered.

Remember to ask **"CAN I, MAY I, SHOULD I"**

When asking your question, word your questions carefully when asking for a response from your Pendulum, ensuring that they cannot be misinterpreted (e.g. "Is this food unsuitable for me?" (at which time? The present, or the future?) The question should rather be "Are there elements in this food which are not suitable for me at the present time? If the answer is "**YES**" go through each item of food for a "**YES**" or "**NO**" response)

Holding your Pendulum as you have been shown, Dowse each item of food in your home. You will be surprised at the answers that you receive.

Do not pre-empt answers from your Pendulum (i.e. do not anticipate "**YES**" or "**NO**") because you will be short circuiting the energy that will be flowing through your energy centres. Instead, try and clear your mind, and open it to the Universe and allow the information to come through the responses from the Pendulum.

WORKING WITH OTHER PEOPLE

Most importantly when working with other people, there are the three things that must be asked.

THEY ARE:

Can I?

May I?

Should I?

It might seem strange that you should ask these three questions, but it is most important before intruding on somebody else's privacy.

Remember to be especially specific in your statements or you will get a **"CANNOT ANSWER"** response.

If you are going to check on another person's health, whether their Chakras are in balance or check their energy field, anything to do with another person, you must first ask permission.

You must make the statement "I WISH TO …………………..

FOR ………….."

(e.g." I wish to check the Chakra's on Joe McDuff now to see whether they are in balance" or "I wish to check Joe McDuff now for illness or injury"

Working with Other People Cont/..

Can I?

Well after getting to know your Pendulum and understanding its responses you will most probably get a "**YES**" answer to this question. If however, you get a "**NO**" response, you will know that at that point in time your expertise does not extend to that level.

May I?

Asking this question clarifies whether it is appropriate for you to find out information about another person and whether you are a suitable person to find out this information.

If you get a "**YES**" answer to this question you know that you are.

If you get a "**NO**" answer to this question, you know that you are not.

Do not be offended if you get a "**NO**" answer. There may be something that you are not aware of about that person. Their personal Spiritual Protection may be such that their Gatekeeper is refusing you access. You may be related, or best friends. There are many reasons why this answer is received. In any case, the "**NO**" response indicates that it is not appropriate for you to receive the answer to your question at that point in time.

Working with Other People Cont/..

Should I?

This may sound like you are repeating the last question in a different way, but I assure you, you are not.

There are many reasons why you would receive a **"YES"** answer to the previous two questions, and a **"NO"** answer to this last one.

Perhaps your patient is not ready to hear the information that you will find out.

Perhaps they are going through some type of Spiritual unfoldment that their Spiritual Guides do not want interfered with.

Perhaps the information that you find out would distress them, or again perhaps it is an invasion of their privacy.

Whatever the reason, respect the answers to your questions.

If you have received all **"YES'S"**, double check your answers by asking: **"AM I CORRECT IN MY UNDERSTANDING THAT I HAVE RECEIVED THE ANSWER "YES" TO ALL MY QUESTIONS?"**

If the answer is **"YES"**, then you can start work.

WORKING WITH CHAKRAS

Chakras are energy centres within the body.

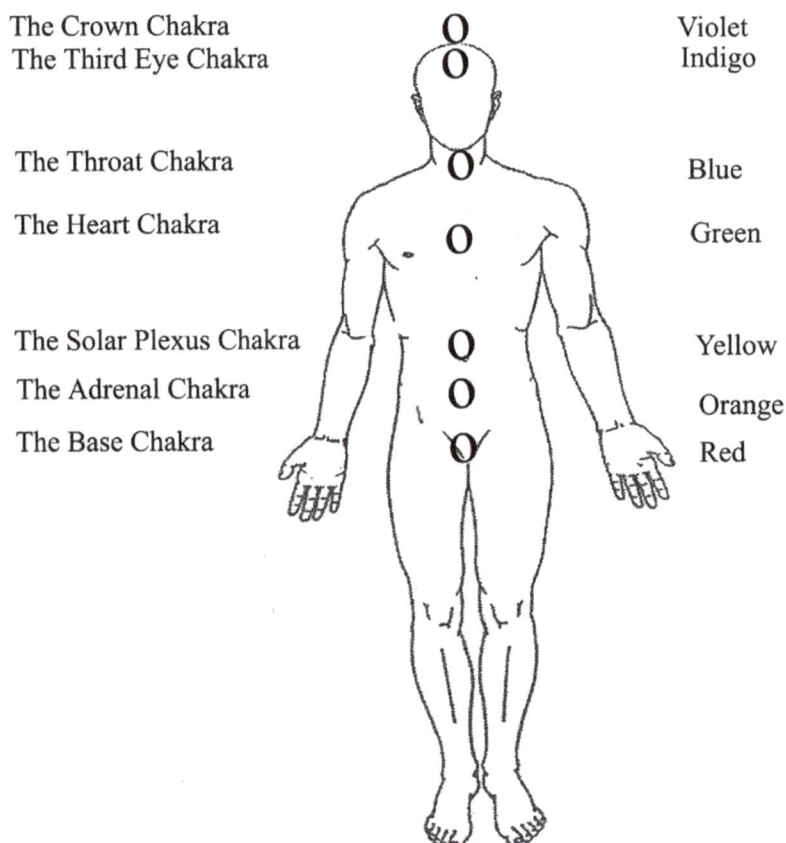

These energy centres can be blocked, out of balance, damaged or even closed. Dowsing these sites, especially on yourself can show you why your life is not going as smoothly as it should.

When these Chakras are not functioning correctly, depression, irritability, anger, lack of self worth are just a few of the feelings that can be experienced.

Working with Chakras Cont/..

The functions for the Chakras are listed below:-

1. **The Base Chakra: "*RED*" This Chakra is located between the genitals and the anus. It is the seat of creativity and ambition. It energises your sense of being of this world. When this centre is blocked or closed, most of the physical vitality is reduced. The individual may suffer from lack of energy, lack of physical presence in his/her personality and the creative processes are significantly reduced. Can also cause depression and lack of self worth.**

2. **The Adrenal (or Sacral) Chakra: "*ORANGE*" This Chakra is located 3 – 4" below the navel. It is the Fight or Flight Chakra. It controls the adrenaline within our bodies. It is the seat of sexuality. When this centre is blocked or closed the individual may suffer from indecision, sexual impairment, frustration, fear and repressed anger.**

3. **The Solar Plexus Chakra: "*YELLOW*" This Chakra is located in the position of the navel. It is the Emotional Chakra. It controls how we interact with people. It is the intuitive (Hunch) area. (The Gut Feeling centre). If this centre is blocked or closed the individual may suffer personality disorders, inability to form lasting relationships and disharmony with those around them.**

Working with Chakras Cont/..

4. **The Heart Chakra: _"GREEN"_ This Chakra is located in the area of the heart. It is the centre of Love and Compassion. If this centre is closed or blocked the individual may experience pain from failed relationships and a fear of giving and receiving love.**

5. **The Throat Chakra: _"BLUE"_ This Chakra is located in the area of the front of the throat. It is the centre of communication. If this centre is closed or blocked, the individual may experience difficulty in expressing their own truth.**

6. **The Third Eye Chakra: _"INDIGO"_ This Chakra is the centre of Spiritual and Psychic awareness. It is the centre from which we perceive our world. If this centre is closed or blocked, our perceptions become distorted and we are unable to tune into the messages we are receiving from our Spiritual Guides.**

7. **The Crown Chakra: _"VIOLET"_ This Chakra is the centre that connects us to the Universe and that creative intelligence that we call GOD. Through this centre we can direct the Divine Light into our bodies. This Divine Light can be asked to cleanse and purify the Chakras. It is this connection that defies Dogma or Creed and becomes 'A KNOWING" If this centre is closed or blocked the individual has difficulty in connecting to their Spirituality and incorporating the Light into their lives.**

Working with Chakras Cont/..

When preparing to Dowse either yourself or another person, it is important to remember to ask those three important questions.

"CAN I, MAY I, SHOULD I"

If the answers to any of these questions is "**NO**" then refrain from Dowsing the Chakras.

If the answers are all "**YES**" remember to ask also the last question.

"AM I CORRECT IN MY UNDERSTANDING THAT I HAVE RECEIVED THE ANSWER YES TO ALL MY QUESTIONS?"

It is then appropriate to Dowse either yourself or another individual.

Holding the Pendulum as you have been shown, Dowse the Chakras in the following order.

1. THE BASE CHAKRA
2. THE ADRENAL CHAKRA
3. THE SOLAR PLEXUS CHAKRA
4. THE HEART CHAKRA
5. THE THROAT CHAKRA
6. THE THIRD EYE CHAKRA
7. THE CROWN CHAKRA

Working with Chakras Cont/..

You will receive the following responses:

1. The Pendulum will not move – this means that the Chakra is **not** open **or** activated.

2. The Pendulum will swing slowly from side to side – this means that the Chakra is open but it is either not activated or is clogged.

3. The Pendulum swings in a circle – this means that the Chakra is open and activated. The rate of swing will indicate how much or how little energy is generated by that Chakra.

You now have the following choices.

1. If the Pendulum indicates that the Chakra is closed, the Chakra must be cleared, opened and activated.

2. If the Pendulum swings slowly or erratically when showing that the Chakra is open but not activated, it will mean that the Chakra is clogged, and must be cleared and activated.

3. If the Pendulum swings slowly or erratically when showing that the Chakra is open and activated, it means that the energy running through that Chakra is low. The Chakra must be energised.

Working with Chakras Cont/..

CLEARING THE CHAKRAS

Bring down White Light through the "**CROWN CHAKRA**". This is connecting with the Universe and the Divine Energy. Envisage that the Light is effervescent (Like sparkling lemonade). Flood each Chakra with this White Light, from the "**CROWN CHAKRA**" down to the "**BASE CHAKRA**" washing out any contamination no matter what the colour, then take the Light down through the soles of your feet. You may need to do this continually for a few moments, to flush out all contaminants into the Ground. It is perhaps wise to ask *"That these contaminants be used as fertiliser for Mother Earth"*

OPENING THE CHAKRAS

After clearing the Chakras, bring the White Light down through the Crown Chakra, flooding each Chakra with White Light as you go down to the "**BASE CHAKRA**".

Focus on the "**BASE CHAKRA**" and visualise it as either a spinning wheel, or an unfolding flower (whichever is easiest for you) Envisage the wheel turning – allow it to turn in whichever way it wants. (The Chakras do not all have to turn in the same direction.) If a flower, envisage the flower unfolding until all its petals are open to the White Light.

Bring this White Light up to each Chakra in turn until you reach the "**CROWN CHAKRA**", whereby the White Light streams out of the top of the head and returns to the Universe.

Working with Chakras Cont/..

ENERGISING THE CHAKRAS

After Clearing and Opening the Chakras, the Chakras are normally energised. However, after long periods of contamination or closure, they sometimes need a helping hand. During periods of stress, illness or grief, the Chakras will also need assistance.

Bring down the Divine White Light through the "**CROWN CHAKRA**" down through each Chakra to the "**BASE CHAKRA**". Visualise the White Light energising and invigorating the "**BASE CHAKRA**". Visualise your wheel or flower being energised and invigorated. Sometimes it is necessary to shut your eyes, hold your breath, and push to get that area pulsating with energy.

Do the same for the "**ADRENAL CHAKRA**". Bring down the Divine White Light through the "**CROWN CHAKRA**" down through each Chakra to the "**BASE CHAKRA**". Then bringing that White Light up from the "**BASE CHAKRA**" into the "**ADRENAL CHAKRA**" Visualising your wheel or flower being energised and invigorated.

Then for the "**SOLAR PLEXUS CHAKRA**". Bring down the Divine White Light through the "**CROWN CHAKRA**" down through each Chakra to the "**BASE CHAKRA**". Then bringing that White Light up from the "**BASE CHAKRA**", through the "**ADRENAL CHAKRA**", into the "**SOLAR PLEXUS CHAKRA**". Visualising your wheel or flower being energised and invigorated.

Working with Chakras Cont/..

ENERGISING THE CHAKRAS Cont/..

Do the same for each Chakra, bringing down the Divine Light into the **"BASE CHAKRA"**, and bringing the energy up through each Chakra to the next one that you wish energised. Returning to the **"BASE CHAKRA"** each time ensures that the energy is running properly up the spine and through each Chakra.

When next you Dowse these Chakras, if this exercise has been done correctly, you will notice that the Pendulum will swing energetically in circles on each Chakra.

You will notice a significant change in your attitude and your energy level. We would suggest that you check your Chakras and follow the above exercises on a regular basis.

As with everything that we teach, the proof is in the doing. We do not have to prove it to you. You will prove it to yourself. Your Pendulum will indicate to you, exactly what it is that your body needs at that particular point in time.

DOWSING FOR HEALTH AND HARMONY

First and foremost we must realise that we are not "The Healers".

All Healing comes from GOD or DIVINE SPIRIT (or whichever name you are most comfortable using for that Divine Creative Intelligence). We are merely the channel through which God may choose for the Divine Healing Energy to flow.

Anybody with a sincere heart and an honest desire to channel the Divine Healing Energy will be used as a vehicle for this Divine Energy to be channelled through their body.

When your patient is either lying comfortably on a healing table, or sitting relaxed in a chair, it is appropriate to offer up a prayer requesting that the Divine Energy be channelled.

"I ask Almighty God (or the Great Spirit or whatever name you call the Great Creative Intelligence we call God) that I be made a pure and uncontaminated channel for the Divine Healing Energy. I ask that whatever is appropriate for this person be given in accordance with the natural law. I ask that my Healing Guides stand close to guide me in this healing"

Dowsing for Health and Harmony Cont/..

Remember to ask those most important questions.

"CAN I, MAY I, SHOULD I"

If the answers to any of these questions is "**NO**" then refrain from Dowsing the body, instead place your hands gently upon the persons body and allow the Divine Healing Energy to flow.

If you have received "**NO**" replies to your questions, understand that this person may be receiving certain aspects of Karma and healing is not appropriate for them.

If the answers are all "**YES**" remember to ask also the last question.

> "AM I CORRECT IN MY UNDERSTANDING THAT I HAVE RECEIVED THE ANSWER YES TO ALL MY QUESTIONS?"

It is then appropriate to Dowse this individual.

Remember to ask your question.

Ask to be shown areas of injury or disease that require healing.

Holding your Pendulum as you have been shown, scan the body slowly, allowing the Pendulum to assume the '**SEARCH**" position. When you come across areas of injury or disease, the Pendulum will oscillate as in the "**YES**" position.

Dowsing for Health and Harmony Cont/..

Record these areas on the Drawing attached with these notes. Confirm with your patient, sites of injury that you have discovered.

After your Dowsing is completed, direct The Divine Healing Energy to those areas.

You may feel a need to rub your hands together or wipe them on parts of your clothing after directing The Divine Healing Energy to parts of the body. This is a natural occurrence, for your hands are passing through the Auric Field of this person, and certain accumulations of energy may need to be removed from your own hands.

Continue directing this Healing Energy until you no longer feel a need to continue.

Remember to: Thank your Healing Guides for assisting you in this matter.

After channelling the Divine Healing Energy for some time, you may no longer need to use your Pendulum. Passing your hand 3" – 4" above the body of the patient will eventually result in you feeling either hot or cold spots where the Healing Energy is required.

ALWAYS BE CAREFUL WHEN GIVING HEALING, THAT YOU DO NOT TOUCH THE PATIENT IN INTIMATE OR SEXUALLY AROUSING WAYS OR IN WAYS THAT COULD CAUSE THE PATIENT DISTRESS.

Dowsing for Health and Harmony Cont/..

Healing can be given with the hands above the body. You do not necessarily have to touch the body for The Healing Energy to be directed. All dis-ease originates in the Aura before manifesting in the body.

Directing The Healing Energy within the Aura is as effective as touching the body. The Healing Energy will go where it is required.

It is not imperative, but it is suggested that the Dowser wash their hands after a healing has been given.

*You may choose to call on **The White Brotherhood** and **Archangel Michael** when commencing your healing but the choice is yours.*

OTHER AREAS FOR DOWSING

1. Herbal remedies (Dowse the Health shops)
2. Libraries (which book is appropriate for me at this time)
3. Maps - for missing people
4. Maps - for areas of significance
5. Maps – for relocation to new dwellings
6. Lost items inside the house.
7. Gardens – for location of new plants
8. Clothing – for suitability – synthetic/natural/etc.
9. Crystals/Candles/Essential Oils/Bach Flower Remedies – which to purchase
10. Food
11. Animals – for health
12. Animals – which to purchase
13. Dwelling Places – which are suitable
14. Motor Vehicles – suitability for purchase
15. Chemicals in the kitchen and garden – which are not suitable.

The list is virtually endless.

We have shown you some areas in which your Pendulum will be an invaluable tool. We leave it now to you, to find out how your Pendulum can assist you in your life and how it creates a link with those Spiritual Guides who surround you.

Dowsing with "RODS"

There are a number of different "RODS" that can be used.

1. The "L" shaped or "ANGLE ROD" made from copper or brass or even a coat hanger.

2. The "Y" shaped "ROD" made from Willow

3. The Curved Cable made from multi strand steel

4. The "Bobber" made from coiled piano wire, wood or even a fishing rod.

Trial and error will show what type of "ROD" is suitable for you.

This Course demonstrates the use of the "L" shaped "ROD".

This "ROD" is normally used in pairs. For our demonstration we use fine brass wire, (approx. ooomm dia.) bent at one end so that there are two identical handles and straight angles. This "ROD" can be held comfortably in the hand. The length and diameter of the "ROD" can be adjusted to your own satisfaction when practicing at home. It has been found by our experience, that the smaller size "ROD" can be carried easily without being cumbersome or obvious.

Dowsing with "ROD"s Cont/..

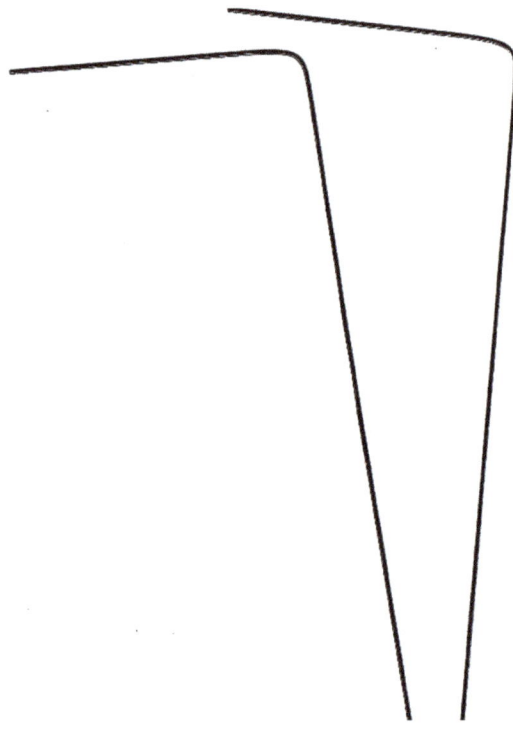

For Safety precautions, we suggest covering the handle so that no sharp edges come into contact with the hands. A length of wooden dowel can be drilled out to place the handle of the "ROD" into, or even a number of wooden beads, with the bottom bead sealed so it remains secure to the handle of the "ROD". These covers should rotate easily, enabling you to grasp them comfortably, while the Divining Rod moves effortlessly within them.

For our experiments the Divining Rods are so small they are not covered.

Hold both Divining Rods in the middle of each palm, thumb covering the forefinger, and not placed on top of the wire. Do not squeeze tight, or the "ROD" will be unable to move.

Dowsing with "ROD"s Cont/..

Hold these Divining Rods at right angles to the body, ensuring that the tops of both are parallel to the ground. If you fail to do this and they point either upwards or downwards even slightly, *gravity* will move the "RODS" to the "FOUND" position.

With some people, the "RODS" start to move automatically as soon as they are ready to start working with them. Do not worry if this does not happen to you. Do not worry if it does, the "RODS" have merely gone into '**SEARCH MODE**' like your Pendulum did.

DOWSING FOR ENERGY FIELDS

To demonstrate how sensitive your Divining Rods are, holding them Parallel to your body, walk up to the person nearest to you mentally asking to be shown the extent of their energy field. When you enter their energy field or Aura, the Divining Rods will either cross in front of you, or point out to either side. Depending on which response you receive, this will be your '**FOUND**' position.

Ask this person to concentrate on their energy field, "pushing it out" as far as they are able. Now Dowse the area again. You will now find that the Divining Rods will indicate a different diameter to the energy field.

Bearing in mind the extent of your own energy field, this simple test will illustrate how often your own energy field will pass through and intermingle with the energy field of another in your daily lives. Walking down the street, sitting on the train or bus, at work and at play. Picking up both positive and negative energies from those you come in contact with.

We don't mind picking up positive energies, but we all dislike picking up negative energies, and it is the negative energies that do the most harm.

The following is an extract from Class Lessons that have been Channelled from Spirit.

Dowsing for Energy Fields Cont/..

"Understand that all things exist of energy. All things exist of vibrations of energy. All things manifest at a different level of vibrations. Each and every thing that exists, vibrating at a level of energy that is appropriate to the species to which it belongs.

Plants vibrate at a particular level. The different species of plants, vibrating at rates that are appropriate for them. Each level of vibration, identifying the gender, the species to which that form of existence belongs.

As vibration is energy, each form of life emanates from this energy, what you call an aura. This aura, showing in its light and level of vibration, the species, the gender, the health, and the emotional atmosphere pertaining to this form of existence.

Because the aura is an energy field operating on different rates of vibrations according to the individual, when auric fields cross or intermingle, as is done so many times a day, it is possible to receive contamination from another's auric field.

Because the level of vibration is unique to the individual, it is also affected by the thoughts emanating from within, and subjected to the thoughts infiltrating from without.

Understand that all thoughts are energy, and when these thoughts are directed toward you, or become part of your auric field, they either add or detract to

Dowsing for Energy Fields Cont/..

the energy within the field. If thoughts of love and kindness are specifically directed toward you, or you are part of a group, that directs thoughts of this level out into the cosmos, and surround this planet, then your vibrations react accordingly, and your auric field flushes with the loving energy. If you are part of a group that directs negativity, or unkind and negative thoughts are directed toward you, or you enter areas where the low level of vibration manifests in large numbers, as in shopping centres, or taverns, then ones auric field responds immediately to the thought forms that are directed or attached to it.

Picture the auric field as a field of vibrating energy that gleams and glistens. If ones thoughts are on a low level of vibration, it dulls and lowers the level of the vibrations, of the auric field until the colours become dense and muddy. If one is surrounded by people of a low level of vibration, then the exterior of the auric energy field, becomes shrouded with thought forms that cover the auric field with a plaque of negative energy, shrouding the colours of the field, and prohibiting the flow of energy within.

If one continually and habitually associates with those of lower levels of vibrations, one eventually builds up a coating around the auric field through which it is difficult to receive the higher levels of vibration in the form of thoughts of love, kindness and spiritual teaching.

This plaque can build up over the lifetime of the individual, until it is extremely hard to penetrate, and

Dowsing for Energy Fields Cont/..

extremely difficult to cleanse.

Each and every auric field is different, and each and every life is different, so it is impossible to estimate on a wholesale scale, the contamination of any one auric field.

Imagine the energy within, trying to flow and emanate when it is coated with negativity from within and without.

To cleanse an auric field, it is necessary to remove the contamination of a lifetime of negativity. This may take some time. If it is done on a regular basis, then it eventually becomes clear, and can be kept so on a daily basis.

Remember always, that when one associates with people of dubious levels of vibration, to remove their contamination by either standing under a shower of light, scraping off the energy particles, or having another do so for you.

It is important to realise that ones emotional responses are directly proportionate to the amount of energy surrounding or attaching to the auric field.

Dowsing for Energy Fields Cont/..

*Quote from Running Deer.
(Running Deer is one of our wise spiritual Guides)*

"Liken the Aura to an immaculate white suit of clothing. Imagine walking down the street of a mining town, where others walk in their mining clothes. How long will it be, before your suit becomes contaminated and dirty. All those who have a knowledge of Spirit, because of the light of their aura, draw to themselves the contamination of others, therefore it is necessary to cleanse and purify the auric field on a regular basis."

The auric field appears egg shaped to those able to see the manifestation of the energy. It appears as a mass of colours, the density and lustre depending on the physical and emotional level of the person whose aura is being viewed.

The appearance of the aura can vary from day to day, and from emotion to emotion, but overall, the balance should remain the same.

Violent emotions can upset the balance of the auric field and disturb the manifestations of colour and energy, so too can drugs, alcohol, and perversity. A lack of vitamins and minerals, weariness, health and illness, deprivation, love, and lack of love, all show within the auric energy field.

Dowsing for Energy Fields Cont/..

The energy being emanated from this auric field can be tapped by those whose lower level of vibration leaves them feeling unbalanced and heavy. Thus can the energy of a high level individual supplant those of a low level individual, so it is at times, you feel drained of energy whilst in the company of others.

The contamination received within ones auric field affects ones own moods and energy, and when the contamination has continued for a great period of time, can lead to complete imbalance of the energy field, and sometimes even illness.

When the contamination is caused by ones own thoughts, the imbalance caused has an even greater affect on ones own health, and can be the greatest cause of dis-ease. Right thinking, and right actions create ease not dis-ease.

The varying thoughts, emotions and levels of vibration that interpenetrate the auric field many times a day, have a distinct and equal reaction on your own auric field.

Remember each time you mix with those of lower levels of vibrations, of the affect those vibrations will have on the auric energy field pertaining to yourself.

It is important to remember, when in doubtful situations, to radiate thoughts of love, compassion and kindness, so that those energies will be absorbed by the infiltrating auric fields. Remember to shine like a beacon in the darkness, giving and drawing on

Dowsing for Energy Fields Cont/..

the limitless power of the Universe. For as these auric fields have interpenetrated your own field, so will yours interpenetrate theirs. And as you will absorb some of their energy, so will they absorb some of yours. In giving and radiating love, you are drawing on the higher energies of the Universe and filling all who come within your sphere with these energies. In thus doing, you will negate any negativity that comes within your field.

You will be unable to tell just whose aura yours has mingled with at any time. It maybe a murderer, somebody who is terminally ill, somebody who is mentally ill, somebody who is lonely, or yet again, somebody who is full of love and compassion, or again one who is a natural healer.

As it takes all types to make a world, so too, does it take all types of auric energy fields to surround these people.

You cannot isolate yourself to prevent contamination, neither can you seal yourself within your energy field, but you can radiate with the knowledge that you have, the healing power that you possess, and the love that lies within. In so doing, you spread a little of the love of the Great Spirit wherever you go. Wherever your auric energy field is touched, you can leave a little love behind."

Dowsing for Energy Fields Cont/..

You now have a perfect example of how wide an energy field can become. You are now aware of how it can intermingle with your own energy field.

As you have learned to Clear, Open and Activate the Chakras with the Divine Light, now use the same Divine Light to Clear your Aura. Flooding your body and your own energy field with Divine Light and removing all contamination and sinking into the Earth as fertiliser for this planet.

Use your Pendulum to now check whether your Aura is now clear. Remember the important questions, **"CAN I, MAY I, SHOULD I"**

Now that you can Dowse an Energy Field, try Dowsing the following:-

1. Dowse the energy field in front of your computer.

2. Dowse the energy field in front of your microwave.

3. Dowse the energy field in front of your television set.

4. Dowse the energy field emanating from your meter box.

5. Dowse the energy field emanating from your power points.

Dowsing for Energy Fields Cont/..

By Dowsing these objects, you will notice that these energy fields vary quite considerably. Some fields of radiation are quite large. Most of these energy fields are quite hazardous, especially the one radiating from your meter box.

1. **Computer.** At our Sanctuary at Craigmore we use a number of Basalt/Amethyst sachets handmade by a friend. These sachets reflect and/or negate the EMF radiation that radiates from certain electrical appliances. If you are able to purchase items such as these locally, we suggest you do so. If not, contact us. Place one of these on top of your Computer and Dowse again. We think it appropriate to place one of these sachets on top of each computer you use, especially those in the workplace.

2. **Microwave.** Basalt/Amethyst sachet. Dowse again.

3. **Television Set.** Basalt/Amethyst sachet. Dowse again.

4. **Meter Box.** Inside the lid of your Meter Box place a triangle of copper wire from the centre top to the bottom two sides. Now Dowse your Meter Box again. If your bedhead is on the same wall as your Meter Box, place one behind your bed as well. Dowse again.

Dowsing for Energy Fields Cont/..

5. **Power Points**. Inside your food packaging packets are plastic covered ties used for sealing the bags. Place one of these around the cord leading into each plug that is plugged into a power point. Twist the tie 2 or 3 times leaving the ends pointing in different directions. Now Dowse your power points again.

As you can see for yourselves, there is an incredible difference in the extent of the energy field of each object after placement of these items.

This is where your Dowsing abilities become incorporated into your way of life. Creating health and harmony in a way that you can readily observe.

We are not telling you to do something that you cannot physically see the results of. We are saying, *"Use the Dowsing skills that you are learning, and see for yourself what happens".*

DOWSING FOR GEOPATHIC STRESS

To cover this subject in its entirety goes far beyond the capacity of this Course.

Briefly:

There are a number of electromagnetic lines that connect to form a grid over the face of this planet. Where lines on these grids connect and/or cross over (especially where your cat likes to sleep) there CAN be areas of dangerous electromagnetic disturbance, and capable of causing illness and disease.

Hartmann Grids:

These were discovered in 1950 by a German medical Doctor, Dr. Ernst Hartmann. He discovered that these lines run North to South, and East to West and extend to a height of approximately 600 feet and 9 inches wide..

The North – South lines appear approximately every 6'6", and the East – West lines approximately every 8'2". These distances can vary a little. This Grid penetrates everywhere.

Curry Lines:

These are a Global network of electrically charged lines running diagonally to the Pole. They are approximately 3 metres apart. This network was discovered by Dr. Manfred Curry and Dr. Wittman.

Dowsing for Geopathic Stress Cont/..

Ley Lines:

These are part of the Earth's energy system. They are like the arteries of the planet. Where ley lines connect, they create power centres which were traditionally used by the pre Christians, as worship centres. These centres were usually marked with a monument or cairn. These monuments today are normally covered with Christian Churches or Temples built where the power centres radiate a universal energy that affects consciousness.

Early civilisations without understanding why, built their roads and cross roads on Ley Lines, following their magnetic influence and power centres.

To discover whether your House and/or workplace is suffering from the effects of Negative energies from any of the above, it is necessary to Dowse the perimeter of the building.

Important: Prior to this exercise you must have on hand a supply of copper water pipe which has been pre-cut into a number of 6 – 8" pieces. A hammer. A number of pieces of wooden dowel with some type of flagging on top.

Dowsing for Geopathic Stress Cont/..

You will find a number of energy lines running through your building. Not all lines will be at right angles.

It is important to mark each energy line as follows.

1. Holding your Divining Rods as you have been shown, walk slowly around the perimeter of your building, mentally requesting that you be shown the lines of energy dissecting your home/work place.

2. Place a flagged marker where your Divining Rod first indicates a line. This shows the side of the energy line.

3. Walk through the line and place a marker where your Divining Rod indicates another line. This shows the other side of the energy line.

4. Turn around and walk back towards your first marker. Your Divining Rod will show the centre of the energy line.

You have now seen that energy lines are like streams. They have a near bank and a far bank, and a centre where the stream is strongest.

5. Ask your Divining Rod which way the stream flows – into your house or away from it.

Dowsing for Geopathic Stress Cont/..

6. Look at the angle in which the stream flows.

7. If it flows towards your House, place a marker at the centre of the stream and remove the other two.

8. If it flows away from your House visualise the angle and where this angle dissects your house. The incoming energy line will be on the other side of your house.

9. Remove the markers and move on to the next energy line.

10. When all energy lines have been marked it is time to produce your copper pipe and hammer which you have previously acquired.

11. Asking the Nature Spirits and Deva's for assistance in what you are about to do, hammer a copper pipe in all areas that you have marked with a flag.

12. Walk around the perimeter of your house with your Divining Rods inside the areas that you have marked to see if there are any lines of energy dissecting your house that you have not already found and marked.

13. **If there are, you must re-check the area again.**

Dowsing for Geopathic Stress Cont/..

14. If there are not, then you have successfully acupunctured the earth for the cessation of negative energy going through your home.

It is now appropriate to go back inside your house, and using both your Pendulum (remembering to ask "**CAN I, MAY I, SHOULD I**") and your Divining Rods check to see that there are no more areas of Geopathic Stress within your home.

Your cat may decide there are more comfortable areas to sleep than on the foot of your bed, but knowing that there are no more harmful energy lines transecting your home it doesn't matter where it now decides to sleep.

We hope that you have enjoyed this course.

*We hope that in some small way
we have been able to assist you in
living a healthier, happier life.*

*We also hope that the skills that you have
acquired today, will grow and develop and
that your journey will have been made a
little easier by the acceptance of these skills.*

*We wish you joy. We wish you
happiness. We wish you luck.*

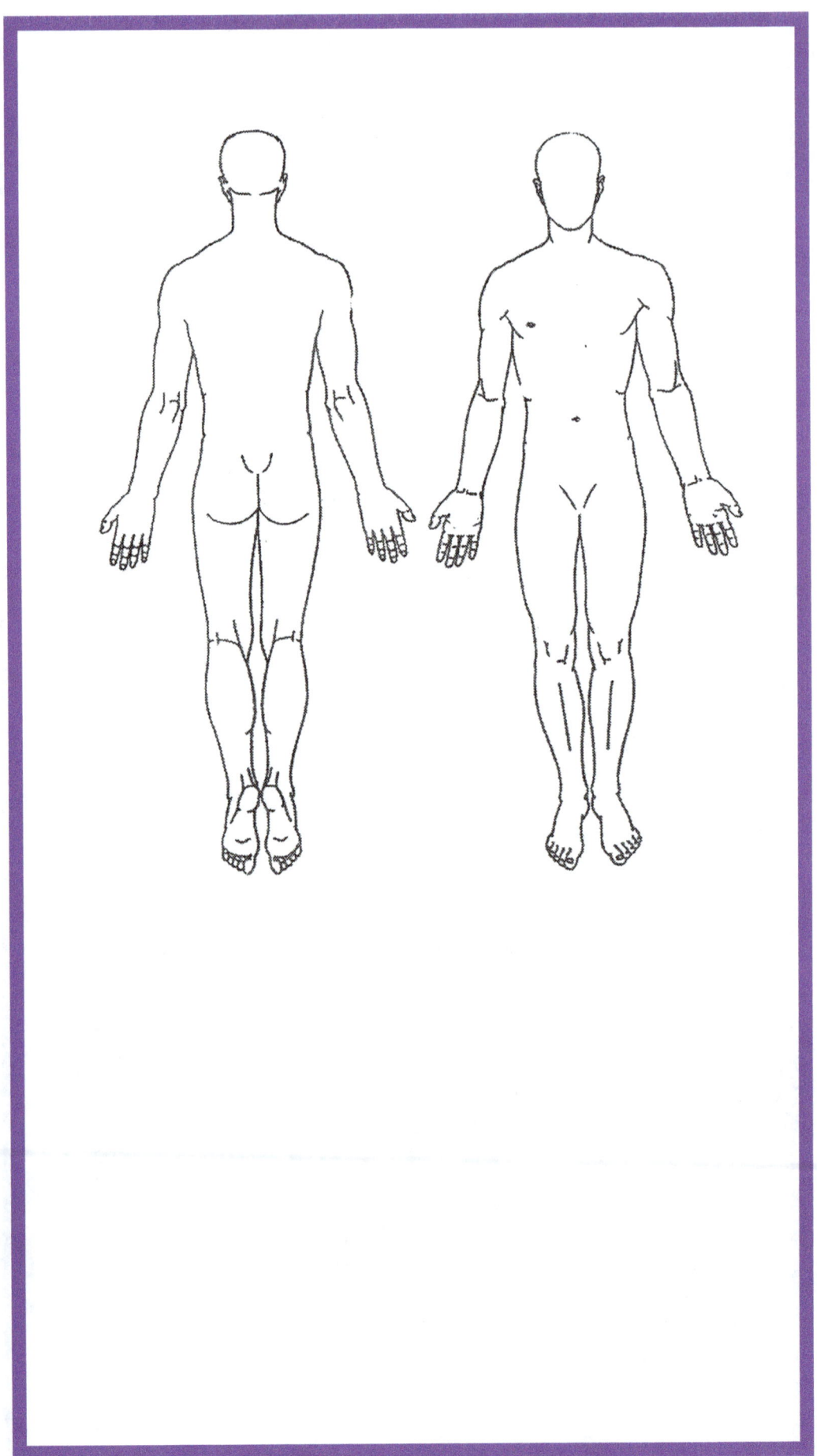

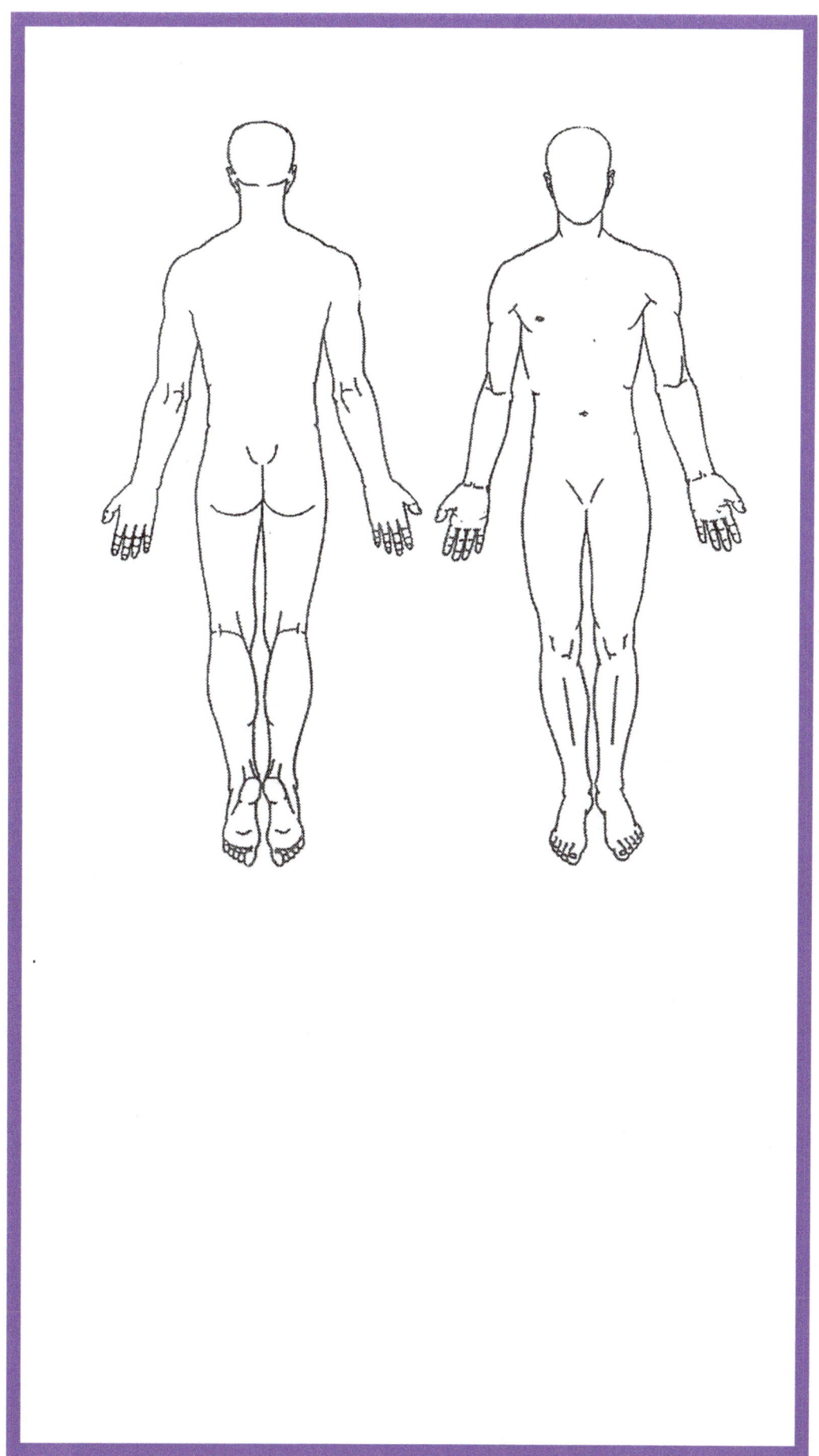

www.ingramcontent.com/pod-product-compliance
Lightning Source LLC
LaVergne TN
LVHW082244060526
838200LV00046B/2051